PETS

MICE AND RATS

Greg Pyers

PEARSON
Heinemann
LIBRARY

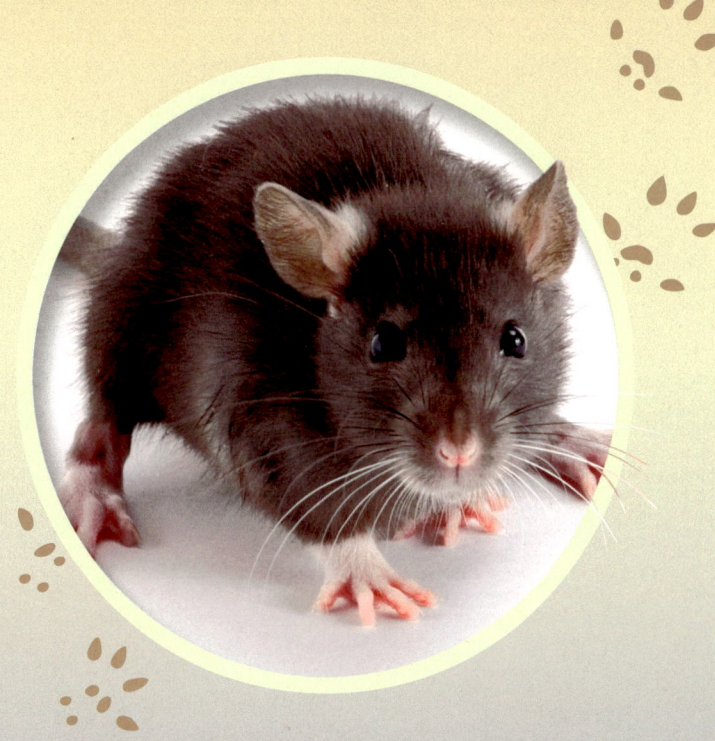

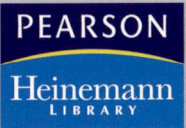

Sydney, Melbourne, Brisbane, Perth, Adelaide
and associated companies around the world

Pearson Heinemann Library

An imprint of Pearson Education Australia
A division of Pearson Australia Group Pty Ltd
20 Thackray Road, Port Melbourne, Victoria 3207
PO Box 460, Port Melbourne, Victoria 3207
www.pearsoned.com.au/schools

Copyright © Pearson Education Australia 2009
(a division of Pearson Australia Group Pty Ltd)
First published 2009 by Pearson Education Australia
2012 2011 2010 2009
10 9 8 7 6 5 4 3 2 1

Reproduction and communication for educational purposes
The Australian *Copyright Act 1968* (the Act) allows a maximum of one chapter or 10% of the pages of this work, whichever is the greater, to be reproduced and/or communicated by any educational institution for its educational purposes provided that that educational institution (or the body that administers it) has given a remuneration notice to Copyright Agency Limited (CAL) under the Act. For details of the CAL licence for educational institutions contact Copyright Agency Limited (www.copyright.com.au).

Reproduction and communication for other purposes
Except as permitted under the Act (for example any fair dealing for the purposes of study, research, criticism or review), no part of this book may be reproduced, stored in a retrieval system, communicated or transmitted in any form or by any means without prior written permission. All enquiries should be made to the publisher at the address above. This book is not to be treated as a blackline master; that is, any photocopying beyond fair dealing requires prior written permission.

Publisher: Sarah Russell
Editor: Cameron Macintosh
Copyright & Pictures Editor: Robyn Formosa-Doyle
Project Editors: Lucy Heaver and Lauren Smith
Production Controller: Jem Wolfenden
Printed in China by WKT Company Ltd.

National Library of Australia Cataloguing-in-publication data:
Author:	Pyers, Greg.
Title:	Mice and rats / Greg Pyers.
ISBN:	978 1 7407 0562 2 (pbk.)
	978 1 7407 0568 4 (hbk.)
Series:	Pyers, Greg. Pets.
Notes:	Includes index.
Target Audience:	For primary school age.
Subjects:	Mice – Juvenile literature
	Rats – Juvenile literature.
Dewey Number:	599.35

Pearson Australia Group Pty Ltd   ABN 40 004 245 943

Acknowledgements
The publishers wish to thank the following organisations who kindly gave permission to reproduce copyright material in this book:
Auscape International Photo Library: 25, 27 (Labat–Rouquette). DW Stock Picture Library: 21 (A. Hampton). Getty Images: 24 upper (Steve Gorton). Pearson Education Australia: front cover and 4, 5, 6, 8, 9, 10, 14, 17 upper, 18, 19, 20, 28, 29 (Alice McBroom). Robert Gott: 11. Istock Photos: 12 (Yang Yu), 13 (Gary Martin), 23 lower (Dan Brandenburg). Shutterstock: title page (Oleg Kozlov), 22 (Maslov Dmitry), 7. Photolibrary: 15, 16 (Alamy–C. Steimer), 17 lower (Tek Image/SPL), 23 upper (Joe Blossom OSF), 24 lower (Superstock), 26 (Mauro Fermariello).

Thank you to George and family.

Every effort has been made to trace and acknowledge copyright. The publisher would welcome any information from people who believe they own copyright to material in this book.

Disclaimer/s
The selection of Internet addresses (URLs) provided for this book/resource were valid at the time of publication and chosen as being appropriate for use as a secondary education research tool. However, due to the dynamic nature of the Internet, some addresses may have changed, may have ceased to exist since publication, or may inadvertently link to sites with content that could be considered offensive or inappropriate. While the authors and publisher regret any inconvenience this may cause readers, no responsibility for any such changes or unforeseeable errors can be accepted by either the authors or the publisher.

The publisher's policy is to use **paper manufactured from sustainable forests**

Words appearing in the text in blue are explained in the Glossary on page 31.

Contents

Introduction	4
Mice and rats	6
Mice and rats as pets	8
Choosing mice and rats	10
Where your mice and rats will live	12
Feeding your mice and rats	14
Exercising your mice and rats	16
Making your home safe for mice and rats	18
Handling and training mice and rats	20
Keeping claws, teeth and hair healthy	22
Going on holidays	24
What to do when your mice or rats are sick	26
Meet my mice	28
Find out more	30
Glossary	31
Index	32

Introduction

Pets are fun. You can play with them, cuddle them or just watch them. You can learn a lot from having a pet: what it does, what it likes and needs, and how to look after it. And it's exciting to see your pet grow.

Having a pet is a big **responsibility**. Your pet relies on you for food, water and a safe place to live. If your pet is sick or injured, it relies on you to make sure it gets proper care.

Different pets have different needs. It is important for the health of your pet that you find out about its special needs and provide for them.

In this series, you will find useful information about six different types of pets – birds, cats, dogs, fish, mice and rats, and rabbits. If you do not have a pet, this information will help you decide which pet you would like to have.

Mice and rats

Mice and rats are **omnivores**, which means that they eat a very wide range of foods. There are many **species** of mice and rats, but only one species of mouse and one species of rat have become popular pets. These are the house mouse and the brown rat. The black rat is common in towns and cities, but it has not become a pet.

House mice and brown rats have lived with people for thousands of years. They have spread across the world from their original home in Asia. After many years of breeding, we now have the tame pet mice and rats of today.

House mice and brown rats still live wild in Australia. These animals are usually grey-brown, but their descendants may be several colours, including white, brown and black.

Mice and rats as pets

Mice and rats make excellent pets. They are easy to care for, and if they are handled regularly, they are very tame.

Mice and rats are social animals, which means that they prefer to live in groups. So, if you want pet mice or rats, get at least two. It is best to get two females or two males. If you get a male and a female you will soon have lots of babies to look after as well.

Mice and rats are curious and like to be active. They live for up to two or three years.

Mice can be a little harder to handle than rats, because they are small and tend to dart around a lot.

Male rats are usually larger and less active than females.

Choosing mice and rats

Before you get mice or rats, you need to be sure that you really want them. You will be responsible for their health. You will have to feed them and clean out their cages regularly.

These animals do not live very long. This may suit you if you are not sure you are ready to look after a pet for many years.

Ask other mice and rat owners about what it is like to have these animals as pets. Ask other members of your family if they will help you look after your mice or rats.

You can buy mice or rats from a pet shop. Choose animals that look alert and active. Their noses should twitch and should be dry, and their eyes should be clear. Their fur should be neat and clean.

Where your mice and rats will live

Keep your mice or rats in a large wire cage. For two rats, a floor 60 centimetres long and 30 centimetres wide is suitable. A cage with ladders and ramps will give your pets plenty of space for climbing. Put the cage on a bench or table in a quiet place away from cold draughts and your pet cat or dog.

Place a cardboard box, a piece of plastic pipe or an upturned plastic flower pot inside the cage for your mice or rats to sleep in. Cover the floor with litter, which can be pieces of paper, paper towelling or tissues. Add some straw for bedding.

Your mice or rats will probably use a corner of the cage for a toilet. This area should be cleaned out every day. You should clean out the whole cage about once a week.

Feeding your mice and rats

Mice and rats can be fed pellets, which can be bought at pet shops. Pellets contain all the nutrients mice and rats need. You can also feed them fresh fruit and vegetables, hay, pasta, yoghurt, wholemeal bread, tuna and brown rice. Seeds and nuts can be fed in very small amounts. These foods have a lot of fat and can make your pet obese.

Your mice or rats must have water available at all times. Water can be provided in dishes or from a drip bottle attached to their cage.

The teeth of mice and rats keep growing all through their lives. If the front two teeth are not worn down by gnawing, they may block the animal's mouth and make feeding very difficult. So, it is important to give your pet food, such as pellets, which wears teeth down.

Exercising your mice and rats

Mice and rats are inquisitive animals, which means they like to explore their surroundings. They like to play with objects. You can make their cage an interesting place so that they can keep themselves busy. You can do this by putting in a rope or a ladder, because mice and rats like to climb.

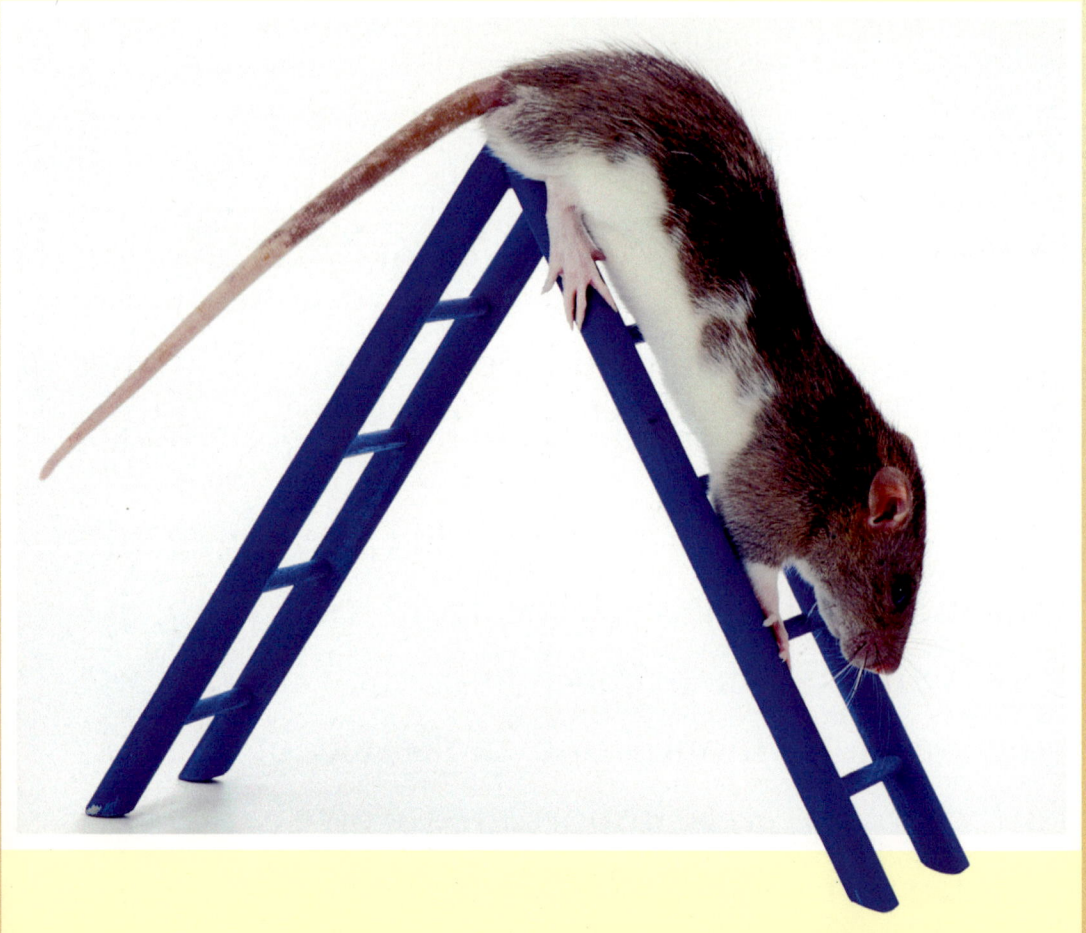

Toilet rolls make interesting toys. Balls, small bells, cardboard boxes and pieces of wood are also good for mice and rats to play with. You should replace these toys from time to time to keep your pets from becoming bored.

Exercise wheels are good for mice and rats to run in when they are in their cage. But, it is a good idea to let your pets out of their cage for a while every day.

Making your home safe for mice and rats

Mice are best kept in their cages, but if you want to let your pet roam free in the house, or in a room, there are dangers. If you get down on your hands and knees, you will see your house from a mouse's or a rat's point of view. From there, look for things that might get your pets into trouble.

Rats like to chew things, including electrical cords. These must be placed out of reach of your pet or it may **electrocute** itself.

Rats and mice get into tight spots, such as behind furniture. You should block off access to these places. And take care when walking around; it is easy to step on your pet!

Handling and training mice and rats

You should handle your mice or rats every day. By doing this, you will make them tame. You should pick up a mouse by the base of its tail and quickly let it put its feet down on your other hand. You can then let the mouse go and allow it to climb over you.

To pick up a rat, place your hand over its back, just behind its head, and lift. Then place it down on your arm.

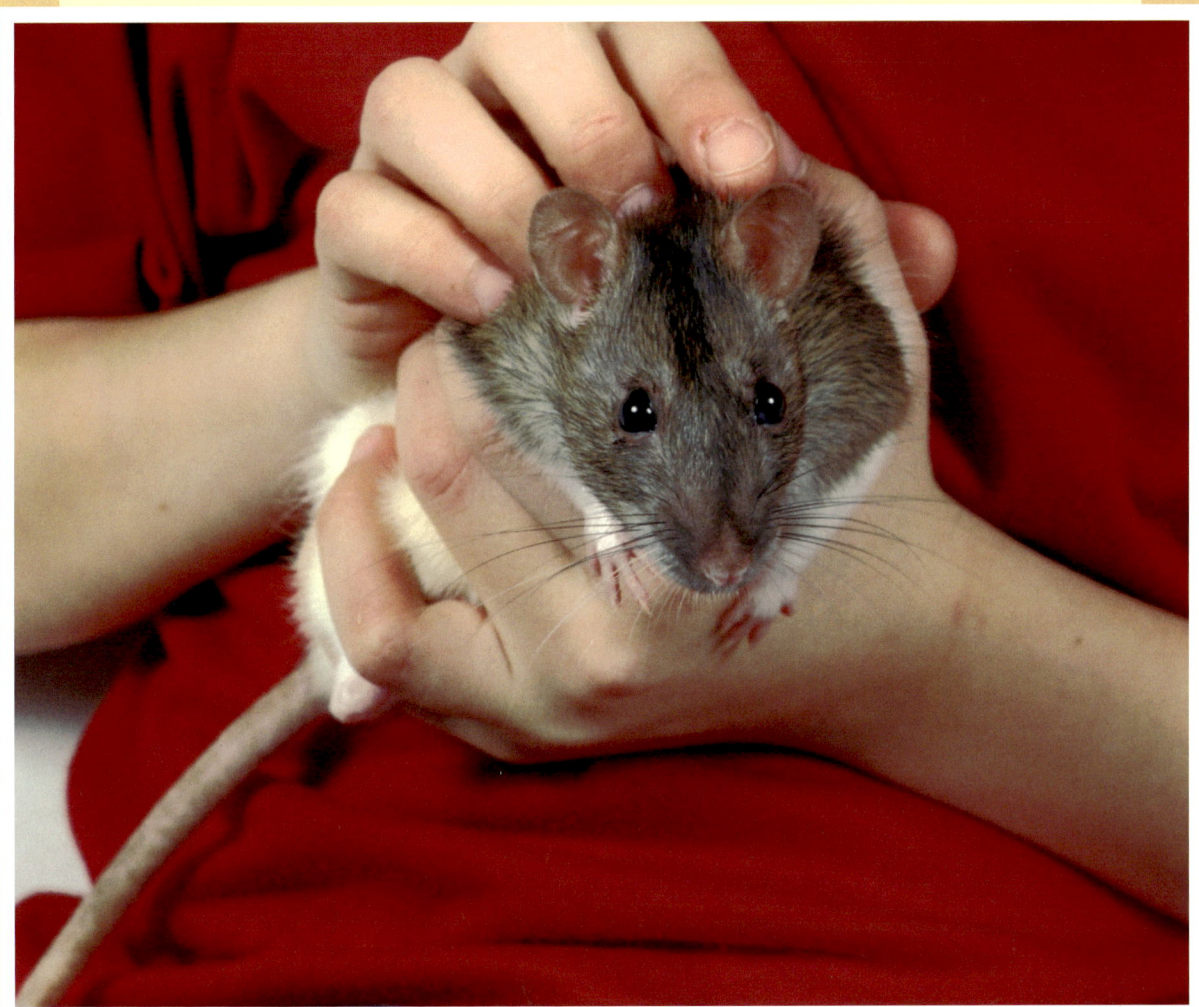

Rats can be trained to use a litter tray. Place the tray on the floor, and when you let your rat out to play, place it in the tray. Every 20 minutes or so, put the rat back in the tray to remind it where the tray is. If your rat uses the tray, praise it with words like 'good rat!' and give it a treat (a nut or a sultana).

Keeping claws, teeth and hair healthy

Rats have sharp claws that grow quite fast. They can get caught in clothing when you nurse your rat, and can scratch your skin. So, every month or so, you will need to trim your rat's claws. Hold your rat firmly, and use nail clippers to nip off the tip of each claw. Mice claws also grow fast but are too small to need trimming.

You should check your rat's teeth to make sure they are not growing too long and causing feeding problems. If you are not sure whether or not the teeth are too long, take your pet to a vet.

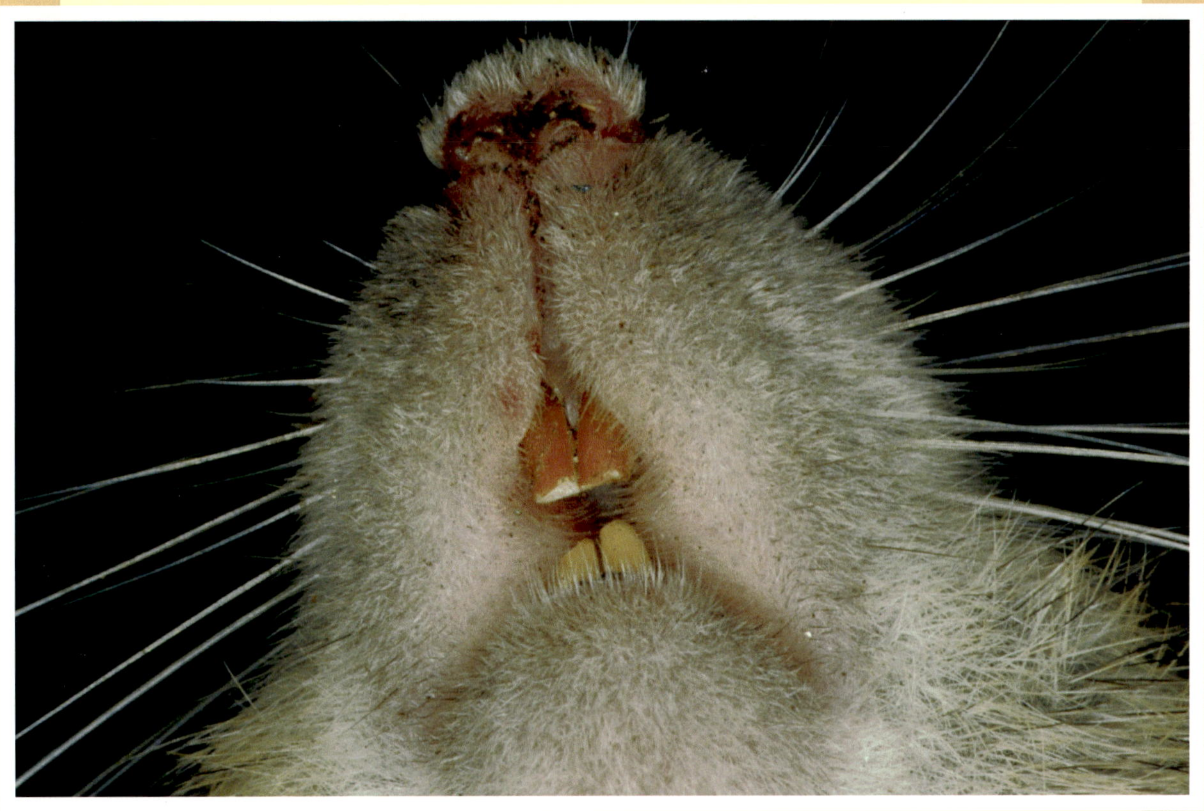

Rats and mice spend a lot of time cleaning themselves. If you keep their cage clean, you will not have to wash your pets.

23

Going on holidays

When you go on holidays, you have to decide what to do with your mice or rats. If you have a cage that has a large feeding tray, you will be able to leave enough food for about a week. Of course, this will depend on how many mice or rats you have. You should make sure the water bottle or bowl is full.

You may have a friend who can visit your house every few days to make sure there is plenty of food available. If you are away for more than a week, your friend will probably have to clean out the cage.

You should give your friend a list of things to do to look after your pets. Whatever you arrange, it would be a good idea to give your friend a gift for his or her work!

What to do when your mice or rats are sick

Mice and rats get sick. Illness can be caused by parasites, which are animals that live in or on your pet. These include lice and mites, which live on your pet's skin.

Mice and rats also get worms. These live in the animal's intestines. Wash your hands after handling your pet because worms can be passed on to humans.

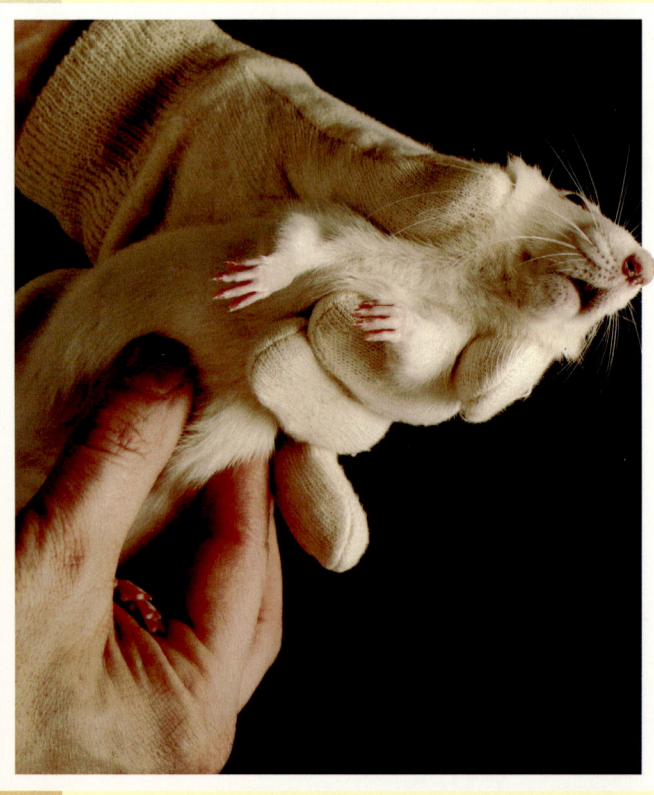

If lumps appear under your pet's skin, your pet probably has cancer. These lumps can be removed by a vet. Cancer is common in mice and rats that are over two years old.

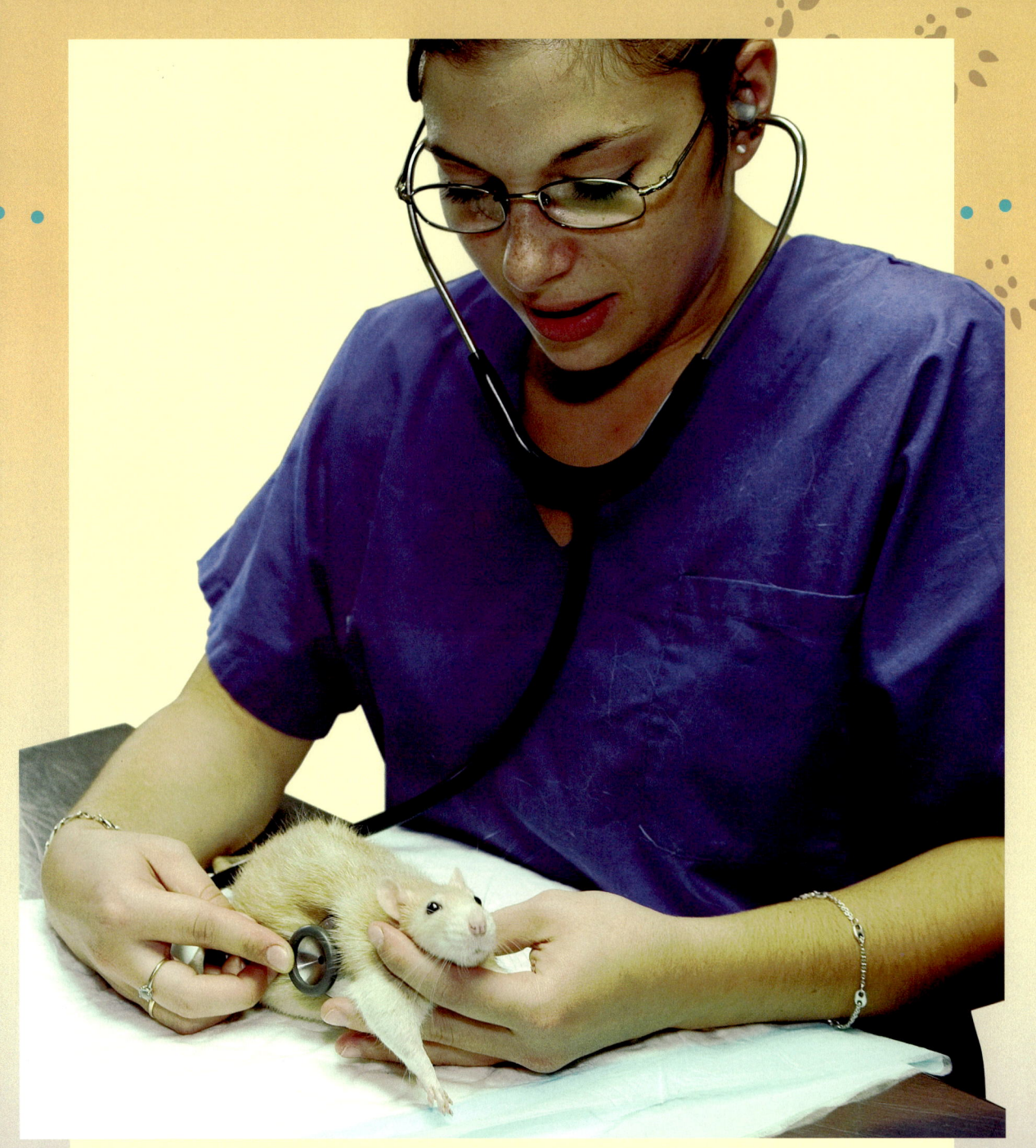

If your pet is sick or has an injury, take it to a vet. When mice or rats get sick, they can be very difficult to treat. The best way to keep your pets healthy is to make sure their cage is clean and that you feed them a healthy diet.

Meet my mice

George has two pet mice, Micky and Dicky.

How old are your mice?
10 weeks.

Where did they come from?
A pet shop.

What do they eat?
Pellets, corn, lettuce, some seeds, a little fruit.

What do you like most about having mice?
They're very quiet and very gentle. They're not very hard to look after. They have a strong smell, but it's not a bad smell. I have to clean their cage only once a week.

Where do they live?
Micky and Dicky live outside in an old rabbit hutch. The hutch has plenty of space for them to explore. The mice make nests in the hay I put in there. On really cold nights, I bring them inside and put them in a cage in the laundry.

What happens when you go on holiday?
We haven't been on holiday yet, but when we do, we'll give them to Grandma to look after. She doesn't know this yet.

Do you have a story about Micky and Dicky?
They like to explore boxes and toilet rolls.

Find out more

Using the Internet

Explore the Internet to find out more about the mice and rats mentioned in this book. Use a search engine such as http://kids.yahoo.com, and type in keywords like 'rats' and 'mice'.

Also, you can visit the Heinemann Library website for links related to this book. The list is regularly updated and can be found at: http://www.heinemannlibrary.com.au/pets

Books

Spilsbury, L. and R. *Keeping Pets – Mice* Heinemann Library, Oxford, 2006

Waters, J. *The Wild Side of Pet Mice and Rats* Heinemann Library, Oxford, 2005

Glossary

descendants children, grandchildren, great-grandchildren

electrocute to kill with electricity

gnawing using teeth to wear away wood, shells or other material

inquisitive likes to explore and investigate

intestines a passage that digested food passes through before it leaves the body

mites small, eight-legged animals

nutrients substances in food needed for good health

obese overweight

omnivores animals that eat many types of food, including animals and plants

parasites animals that live in or on other animals

responsibility something you have to do

social lives in groups, likes company

species a type of animal

Index

A
Asia 7
Australia 7

B
black rat 6
brown rat 6, 7

C
cages 10, 12–13, 15, 16, 17, 18, 23, 24, 25, 27, 28
cancer 26
claws 22

D
dangers 18–19

E
exercise 16–17

F
food 4, 6, 14–15, 24, 25, 28

H
hair 23
handling mice and rats 8, 9, 20–21, 26
holidays 24–25, 29
house mouse 6, 7

I
illness 26–27

L
lice 26
litter 13, 21

M
mites 26

O
omnivores 6

P
parasites 26
pet shop 11, 14, 28
pets 4–5, 6, 8, 10, 11, 12, 25

S
social animals 8
species 6

T
teeth 15, 23
toys 17

V
vet 23, 26, 27

W
water 4, 15, 24
worms 26